Beautiful Girl

Extraordinary stories from my last 12 days
with Española's Purple Lady, Rosalía Triana

by Melissa J White

Acknowledgments:

Tribute by Melissa J White and *Rosalía Triana - A Life Story* by Robert Tomlinson were originally published in the *Abiquiu News*, 2023.

Photo of Rosalía Triana by Eve Andrée Laramée
Cover photo by Roksolana Zasiadko, Unsplash

ISBN: 979-8-9897572-1-3

Facing Pages Publishing
Santa Fe, NM
facing-pages.com
facingpagesinfo@gmail.com

for Rosalía Triana
December 13, 1946 – December 1, 2023

Datura seeds spill
    from a long white envelope–
the heart of winter

Foreword

I met Rosalía Triana in 2008 at the New Mexico Filmmakers Intensive. We were both in the screen-writing track. When her film, *Epi's Dilemma*, was made, she asked me to design the postcard. When I got my first job as a script supervisor, she taught me how to score a script in two hours in a little cafe in Española. When I made my short film, *Wastewater*, she was my scripty. She encouraged me to start a writing class and she came every Sunday for two years, only missing those days when her students were performing. I built her websites; she interpreted my childrens' birth charts. Over the last 15 years, we would help each other on as many film, writing and creative projects as possible. Her voice was always full of laughter and generosity.

When I heard she was in the hospital and was refusing medical intervention, I was grief-stricken, but not completely surprised. For the last two years she talked about the end of her life directly and in metaphor. She drove the 40-minutes to my house one day and gifted me with a beautiful turquoise and shell necklace, saying, I want to give this to you while I still can. She did this with others, too. She told me she loved me at the end of most of our phone calls and classes.

I spoke with her friend, Marta, and the family, and they agreed it was OK if I posted the updates they were making to Rosalía's Facebook page so others would know and not be too surprised. While I did that, I also began to visit her in the hospital, and came away enjoying the time, while learning how to grieve on a day-to-day basis. I began writing posts and sharing them every day about what I was experiencing. In this way, her family and others who could not visit her in person were able, in some small way, I hoped, to be by her side in her last moments.

I went with her on the transport when they moved her to a hospice in Santa Fe. I'd made arrangements with her family and the hospice staff to let me know of any changes that would indicate her imminent passing, and I was the first person they called when she went.

Rosalía often spoke of synchronicity—she would defend its existence, I would defy it, all in good fun. On the last Monday she was in hospice, I bought a small, hand-made, electric birch tree with lights on the tips of the branches. I added AA batteries and placed it on the bay window/altar where others were leaving vases of deep red flowers, purple star balloons, seeds, photos, and even the last pair of boots she bought—faux purple snakeskin Doc Martens.

Each night the little tree would turn on at 7:01 pm and turn off six hours later. That Friday night, one of her caregivers was in her room when the tree lit up. They were saying goodnight to a final visitor. Minutes later, Rosalía took her last earthly breath.

I could have added batteries and turned on that tree any time on Monday, yet I did it exactly four days before she died, nearly to the minute. There are 1440 minutes in a day—you do the math, but I think the odds of her dying just as the tree was lighting are about one in 3 million.

Rosalía believed in synchronicity, but I believe she was the embodiment of it herself by connecting people at exactly the right time in their lives to the very thing they loved most.

The birch tree is now on my altar reminding me of Rosalía's magic at 7:01 pm every evening.

Melissa J White, December 10, 2023

Friday, November 17, 2023

Hello, many friends of Rosalía! I have been given an OK from her family to post updates here on her Facebook page.

If you have not yet heard, I am sorry to tell you that Rosalía is in the hospital at this time. She suffered a severe heart attack on Sunday night, and her good friend/landlady, Marta, knowing and having worked with Rosa's healthcare wishes, helped her to receive pain care at a hospital where she is currently in the ICU. Marta and the family ask that we please do not call or come by the hospital as it is overwhelming for Rosalía and puts a lot of demands on the small, Española ICU staff. (Not to mention Covid making everything worse.) Rosalía's heart is still very strong and she hopes to come home soon.

What you can do is post here on her Facebook page and Marta will share these messages and photos with her. I will post Marta's update each evening so you are informed.

We love you, Rosalía, Our Lady of Purple! We wish you great energy and comfort.

- Love from Melissa

Day 1
Monday, November 20

I went to visit my friend Rosalía in the hospital today. I stayed all day with her. When I left, my heart was full. Not full of grief, not full of joy, just full of being in her presence.

For most of us, it's hard to visit someone in the hospital. We feel awkward with the silences and the suffering of our family and friends, their bodies acting independently of their wishes.

With my friend Rosalía, I had to accept that she was ready to go. It helped me to hear from her caregiver, and from the ICU nurse that she had told everyone when she was admitted after her heart attack that she did not want further medical care. I looked back on the last two years and identified many times when she spoke about being ready to go. Once I understood her wishes, I was able to separate my own needs from what she needed.

What was amazing as she slipped in and out of awareness was that when she was there with us, she was exactly herself. Witty, funny, loving. When I gave her a hug upon entering her room she said, "You smell good. You smell just like you." Later she looked me right in the eye and said, "Wabi-sabi!" I laughed so hard. I lived in Japan for a year, and the philosophy of wabi-sabi was something I wrote about many years ago. For her to pull that out was fucking fantastic because it's not, in my opinion, that she is delusional during this time; it's that she takes a break from being in this reality and is popping over to the next reality. She is lucid and translucent. I would mention people who were leaving her loving wishes on her Facebook page and she would remember them and repeat their names.

In the middle of the afternoon I gave her friend Marta a break and sat with Rosalía while she mostly slept. The machine noise of the bed in the room was incessant so I brought out the drum I had borrowed from my daughter and began a light rhythm. I discovered, not being any kind of drummer at all, that to tap a drum once, just right, you achieve a beautiful, shivering garden of sound resonating along the drum head. But in order to continue the beat, you have to tap a second time and that next tap stops the resonance of the first tap. The metaphor was not lost on me: to continue a beautiful sound, the first note has to stop.

So my rhythm was a big tap and a slight pause to hear it and three small taps. It was hypnotic and pushed away the machine noise. The light drumming was like a sound thread connecting Rosalía, the clouds outside the tall windows, the empty halls, and the green jello on her bedside table.

As a nurse came in to check on her, she leaned against the bed and the loud mechanical noise that had been jarring my nerves all day simply ceased.

Day 2
Tuesday, November 21

I don't know if it's the morphine, or her life-long studies of the transitions between worlds, but Rosalía had some interesting *bon mots* today.

Sitting next to her bed, she tells me, You should see the light on your face. So I told her I would take a picture but that the light was a reflection of her.

She drifted off but when she came back, she said excitedly, I just died!

You did?

Yeah!

What was it like?

It's open. So open.

The other side? I asked.

Yeah! I am opening still.

I tell her, You are teaching me so much. You have taught everyone. But you can stop teaching now.

Wooo! She says another time, like she's on a roller coaster. That was magical!

It was?

Yeah, she says in awe.

Your eyes are purple, she says looking at me deeply.

I've been wearing purple every day, I say. Today I'm wearing a purple jacket. Yesterday I wore a purple shirt. But you have purple hair. You branded yourself with purple.

She laughs and says, Yes I did. I say, In your next life, we will know each other by the color purple.

When I sit down next to her she calls me, Beautiful Girl.

But, I discovered, she calls most people the same.

Day 3
Wednesday, November 22

Today was the day my friend Rosalía would be transported from the Española hospital to a hospice house in Santa Fe. I asked the family if I could ride in the transport with her. It would be up to the EMS driver and I let them know it was OK if they said no. They explained that there was no place for me to sit except in the passenger seat in the front; I wouldn't be able to sit in the back with her, I wouldn't be able to see her. I said, that's fine. I'll sit up front.

Moving her onto a gurney caused her a lot of pain, but she also had a lot of drugs "on board." As we exited the hospital, I told the driver, a young paramedic born and raised in Española, If the worst happens, can you stop for a moment? He looked at me and nodded.

We drove through the small town and up the hill, and I said, Rosalía, you're leaving Española. It was a solemn journey, and I thought of Emily Dickinson's poem where she describes a last carriage ride around the town.

Because I could not stop for death / He kindly stopped for me…

I didn't realize until I was riding along, that what I was doing was bearing witness. I wondered at the source of my desire to do this. I couldn't alleviate her pain; she felt every bump, no matter how carefully and slowly the vehicle went. I couldn't look into her eyes to say, Beautiful Girl, or crack a joke. So, why was I here?

When my mother died, it just felt wrong that they put her in a body bag, zipped it up, and took her away with no one to be next to her. Since then, I have felt the need to sit next to my loved ones on their way out. When my Zen friend Robert died, we chanted the heart sutra as his body entered the flames, and sat in meditation for the time it took his body to turn into ash. Tears streamed down my face for hours. Very dramatic!

Rosalía made it to Santa Fe and is now in a cozy beautiful room with a big window for her to see tall trees and lots of sun. I stayed for a while as the family managed the paperwork and every time her pain woke her up I looked into her eyes. Beautiful Girl, I said. I also made her laugh by telling her she had more drugs in her system than she has ever had, that she was flying high. Unable to form words, she gave me a big smile.

I told her how many people love her and are thinking about her. I read more posts people left on her page. Then I had to stop.

I crossed my arms over the side of her bed rail and put my chin on my hands and for the first time in three days, I shed tears. The reality of her leaving comes in waves and I had kept a tsunami at bay too long.

But who is to say how long she has? I imagine at night when it's dark, and no one is around, she will sit up in bed and climb over to the window seat and stare up at the stars.

I let her family know I'd be back in the morning. Then I dutifully practiced self care by catching the last afternoon shift at La Choza and enjoying a hot plate of red chile chicken enchiladas and a St. Rita margarita in Rosalía's honor.

Cheers, girl!

Day 4
Thursday, November 23

One thing I learned from giving birth to three children is that each birth is different because each child is different. I'm beginning to think that way about death as well. Each death is different, depending on the person who is dying.

Rosalía's spirit is radically inclusive. In talking with some of her friends at her bedside, we reiterated: that girl just wants to have fun. And she wants to have fun with *you.*

I spent some time with Rosalía today and it hurt me to see her so unresponsive. Her breathing is shallower and she only showed a small amount of recognition. She is so far down the rabbit hole, it's hard to reach her and you just want her to sleep peacefully so you try not to make too much noise. Her lovely caregivers say she was talking in the morning, but by the time I visited in the afternoon with my sister, also a friend of the Purple Lady, the aware-ness in her eyes was gone. We opened a window so her spirit could find its way out.

It's hard to admit all the feelings I had today. I wanted her to go so she could move on to her next adventure and be free of her struggle to exist.

But I also didn't want to admit how sad I will be when she's not in my writing class come Sunday. When I can't gab with her on the phone in the evening. When I can't ask her, WTF was that? about any topic at all.

But I'm also learning that my journey through these days is a heightened awareness of just how good life is. Because whatever Rosalía went through growing up, it made her a person that encouraged and protected the creative spirit in others, even when she questioned her own value. I think of her as accepting life as good without a drop to waste.

During the last couple years she was in my class, more than once she asked me if what she was writing was at all interesting. And even though I tried to tell her that stories about a wild, pixie girl actor in NYC in the '80s delving into past life regressions was always highly entertaining, she didn't always believe me. I finally asked, why don't you think they are? And that became a koan for her—a question without an answer.

Before I knew she'd had a massive heart attack, I had decided for the first time in decades, not to cook dinner on this day of national gratitude. I just decided to stop making my life so complicated. So we had reservations for an early dinner at La Casa Sena and I was looking forward to it.

Sitting across from my younger sister and my oldest son, drinking a pumpkin white Russian, their eyes shine back at me as we talked and joked.

For a fraction of a second I wondered, how can I be laughing so much when my friend is lying in a bed, unable to laugh anymore? And the image I received as an answer was that the light that was fading from her eyes was shining in mine, and that light was shared with others.

If anyone can shatter into ten thousand shining pieces of purple glitter when they leave this mortal coil, to rain down on all our heads and give us the gift to love the creative spark we all have, it will be Rosalía.

Day 5
Friday, November 24

I'm sitting here with Rosalía as she breathes. When I match my breath to hers, it is light and special and slower than yesterday.

I am no Rosalía. I am just me. But what I can say about being with Rosalía in these days is this:

I hope we do not suffer too much during this time. Life is not about suffering. I know, I know. There is a long-standing tradition of quoting the Buddha that, "life is suffering." But I once read an article in *Tricycle* magazine that changed my mind. This writer came to a different meaning about what that phrase meant.

Suffering is life.

That doesn't mean all of life is suffering all the time. It means, rather, that suffering is life, loving is life, grief is life, joy is life, irritation is life, and even dying is life.

We have to grieve, it's part of life.

Also, grieving is different for everyone. It will look different from the outside and the inside. Someone who is angry, someone who jokes a lot, someone who cries a lot, someone who is stoic— can all be grieving.

When I was leaving to drive to Española to be there when the transport team came to pick up Rosalía to drive her to the hospice in Santa Fe, they told me the transport would not arrive before 9 AM. I was late getting ready to leave and rushing around, and I kept losing things—my water bottle, my glasses, my cat. Seriously, I couldn't find my cat when I was going out the door and I had to search my house to make sure he was still inside. (He was.) During this time, I was stressed out, getting angry, worried I would be too late… I was grieving. Finally, I just said, *Rosalía, if you have to go, go. I'm fine. We are fine.*

I have found myself doing that all this week even just visiting her for a few minutes when I feel rushed and I won't get there in time before she passes, I have come to a place where I am OK with that. I am already at peace.

I know once she goes I will have a different kind of grieving, but for now, she has taught me not to suffer more than I have to. Things will happen in their own time. I cannot make her stay, I cannot make her leave. It's her and her body's decision.

Time doesn't heal anything in and of itself. You are healed in time. For me, a deep grief might take a year for me to be back to balanced, but I will still feel the grief. And I feel grief differently for different people that have died.

I hope my words have been of benefit for you through this grief of losing Rosalía. (Disclaimer here that I am no therapist but support mental wellbeing.)

One thing people have said often to help during the

grieving process is to light a candle. I remember a moment from when I was very young and my grandfather passed. I was in my aunt's house in Kentucky and they lit a candle for him and left it in the room where he had died. They told me the light *was* my grandfather. Maybe they called it his soul or his spirit. I found myself focusing on that flame and thinking he was somehow transformed into the light. Beginning of my empiricist nature.

I'm grateful that my aunt kept that practice and initiated me into it because looking back now so many years later, I can say that the beauty of a candle is a wonderful way to focus when you're grieving.

I have one of those electric candles with wax and an AA battery that turns it on at sunset. When Rosalía became sick, I turned it to stay on all the time, telling myself that when she passed, I would turn it back to sunset again. I find small rituals like this help me be in a gentle space with an open heart.

Perhaps find a small action to do for yourself to honor Rosalía's life for when you hear that she has passed. Later you can make it a big beautiful action. In the spirit of the Rosalía you knew, put on Cyndi Lauper and dance. Call a friend. Dye your hair purple.

Or just gaze at a candle and feel the love she had for you and how synchronistic it was for you to have met her when you did.

Day 6
Saturday, November 25

Here in Rosalía's room at the hospice this evening. The sky is flat pink behind the snow-laden piñon. Some-one has left two purple star balloons. So Rosalía.

I spoke to her a little, relaying names and love. Sometimes she smiled big in recognition. Other times she wrinkled her brow and looked at me as if to say, Who the fuck is that?

Six inches of snow overnight delayed my visit to the hospice this morning. I was at the sink washing coffee cups when I had a ghost thought—one of those thoughts you have after someone dies, forgetting that they're gone. *I have to tell Rosalía…*the thought begins, but then you realize that soon you won't ever get to tell Rosalía anything again.

These thoughts come from the neural pathways that are deeply grooved into our brains and hearts by habit over time. The idea runs down the track until it suddenly hits the brick wall of reality and the excitement of the thought bounces back. It's that bounce back that hurts the most— the sharing impulse realizes it's alone.

My sister and I shoveled out our cars and the top of the driveway and she was on her way back home. The sun was glistening off the snow and the sky was bubblegum blue. Birds were psyched to knock snow off branches in their games.

I put the snow shovel against the side of the house, grabbed my coffee and walked around through the gate to the back of the house and sat looking out at the pristine blue white snow covering my backyard, filling the bird-bath. Water dripped from the roof and the umbrella, a rhythmic falling of melting snow, dripping and splashing at my feet.

When my daughter was little, she loved the snow melting off the roof. She would get pots and pans and buckets and tea cups and put them underneath each drip, each splash of melting ice. Obviously, then as now, we had no gutters. When she was done adjusting her pieces, she would sit back and listen. She called it a woozy-walky.

It was a kind of environmental musical instrument. In her mind, she could've meant something else. Maybe she meant water walking. She often had names for things when she was little that seemed to come from a past life vocabulary, judging by the certainty with which she said them.

I spent some time outside listening to the sounds of snow melting, allowing my mind some space to begin to develop new neural pathways.

Day 7
Sunday, November 26

R osalía's family posted this last night:

The family wants to give this Sunday evening update
to all of the lovely friends of Rosalía.

You may know that Rosalía is in Scott's House Hospice
in Santa Fe. The compassionate care and comfort that
she is being given is superb. The place itself is perfect. We
are keeping in constant contact with the staff, and it is so
gratifying that they love her already. Of course, right!? One
of the night nurses recognized her, and had goosebumps as
she realized that she knew Rosalía decades ago, when she
had been helped by Rosalía. Typical.

Rosalía has moments of lucidity in which she can recognize the staff and even visitors she has not seen in a long
time. She's non-verbal, but her magical eyes and sweet
crooked smile speaks volumes! Rosalía had previously
had some breakthrough pain, and seemed to be agitated
at times. That part of the journey is over. And now, she is
beautifully peaceful and serene.

Her Hospice Doctor has spoken to us in length about our
purple lady. She has said that she wishes that when she
herself passes, she will die as gracefully as Rosalía. There is
no actual way to know when Rosalía's wish will be granted,
but it will not be long. In the meantime, she is patient

Sigh.

Ambercare Hospice is providing her medical needs and final arrangements. Rosalía put the plans in place to donate her body to science.

If you care to donate to Scott's House, please visit the link to the website. We are blown away by the volunteers there, who selflessly travel long distances and spend so many hours there, out of their pure love of service to the dying. Hospice workers are angels here on earth.

Please post if we can answer any questions you may have. We can't really even comprehend the amount of lives Rosalía has touched, and we are honored to call her sister.

Terry Safranek, Steve Traina, Patty Jean

Day 7
Sunday, November 26

I'm home from visiting Rosalía this evening and some-where in purple hazy, Rosalía-land, where she resides right now, she has had to learn how to communicate in a whole new way.

I noticed that she would smile, and then quickly drop her smile. She would furrow her brows, then unfold them. She would raise one eyebrow. She would raise both eyebrows. She would wrinkle her nose like Samantha in *Bewitched*. And in between these gestures, she would retreat back into a place of rest.

I brought the caregiver on duty in, someone who knew Rosalía years ago, of course. I asked the caregiver to watch her as I talked to her, and I said, I think she's saying, Yes when she wrinkles her nose. And then Rosalía wrinkled her nose.

And we were off to the races!

I've only been with or near four people when they've passed and one of the hardest things is to know how to help them during this process. What do you say? It seems so awkward to talk to someone although now I have se-curely learned that people in this state can hear you, and in Rosalie's case, can hear you very well. So, having a level of communication was honey to my soul.

I asked her, Rosalía, do you want me to read to you? Nose wrinkle. You read T*he Tibetan Book of the Dead* to Leo when he was dying. Do you want me to read that to you?

Nose wrinkle.

I chose the Robert Thurman translation of the book and downloaded it to my phone. I picked Thurman because when I was living at the Zen Center in San Francisco and at Green Gulch, I used to see his talks and loved his energy.

The first thing to know about *The Tibetan Book of the Dead* is that the title is a marketing ploy. It is better translated as, *One Way to Learn about One of the In-between States*. (My paraphrasing.) How on earth do you read a book about dying to a person who is dying? But Rosalía did it, so I dived in.

I started with the introduction, where Thurman says this translation is a how-to guide, really, for the regular person who may not understand 14th century hierarchies of evil and kind deities that one might meet in the Bardo. And the important part is to be able to tell the person what is happening right after they've died because they will be hanging around wondering what to do.

Glancing at Rosalía, I stopped reading. Having only dipped into this book in years past as a curiosity, I decided I would need to go home and do a crash course on it just to get my bearings. Until then I looked for another book to read out loud and settled on a graphic novel version of *To Kill a Mockingbird*. As I read the tiny type and looked up at Rosalía she was resting very calmly.

When it was almost time to go at 8 PM, I went back to speak with the caregiver and share a few stories. She had worn purple sneakers to work that day just for Rosalía.

As we were chatting, I had the sudden thought that maybe when Rosalía wakes up confused and doesn't know where she is, maybe she doesn't know she's dying. I asked the caregiver what she thought. We've all been telling her it's OK to go, but are we being specific enough? Have we told her where to go exactly? Rosalía isn't Buddhist in the strict sense but maybe she needed this kind of guidance.

My work with Rosalía these past few years with her writing has been so much fun and we are so what-the-fuck about it, if you know what I mean. She's going for it. She keeps saying she's going to finish these two books and she very nearly did it. So we have a very straightforward and fun relationship. Based on that, I decided I could tell her, just in case she doesn't know by now, that she's dying. If it was me, and I kept waking up confused and unable to move or talk, I would want to know so I could be prepared. I took a deep breath, and said to the caregiver, OK, I'm going to go do it now.

I went back to her bedside and said her name, and her eyes flickered open, and her question came into her face again.

I said something like this:

Rosalía, we all love you so much. Your family your friends are all around you. You are safe and you have lived the life of a mischievous bodhisattva. But now it's time for you to go. You are dying. Do you understand? You are going to leave this life and what a life it's been! You have left so many people happy and fulfilled and inspired your entire fucking life. You won't forget this life. But now you need to be prepared to die. (Dear god, shades of *The Princess Bride!*) *I'm here to help you, your family is here to help you, all your friends are here to help you and the caregivers are here. We love you and we are all making plans to see you again in the next life.*

My voice was not loud, but direct, the way I've seen my sister talk to patients who are confused. I also felt like I was reciting that Buddhist chant:

All my ancient, twisted karma
From beginningless greed hate, and delusion
Born from body, speech and mind
I now fully avow.

She was smiling at the beginning of this speech, but her eyes were closed, and she was listening by the end. I got my coat, gloves, hat, all the necessities to stay warm, blew her a kiss and walked out under the full moon to my car.

I sincerely hope I have not caused her any more suffering. And if I have, she can always get me back in the next life.

Day 8
Monday, November 27

The moon woke me up at 6 AM this morning. As bright in my room as the sun. I was on Rosalía-time all day. Got to visit with more of her friends and family, cleaned up the altar where people have been leaving gifts of flowers, gems, incense, balloons, and a little Christmas tree with purple peace ornaments—my addition.

She is still recognizing people, her breathing seems the same.

My mission today was to find a purple scarf to drape around Rosalía's neck and I failed. I went to three different stores all the while noting that purple is not a Christmas color and everybody's getting ready for Christmas.

In the end, I realized that the deep purple blouse I was wearing was exactly what would look good around her neck. So I bought a little lavender sweater from Target and went back to the hospice and traded my silky shirt for the sweater. I gave the shirt to the caregiver and asked if they could make it look nice like a scarf, and it was beautiful on her. It was like one of those Roman statues with drapery; she looked very royal and in her element.

And during the day I was not unhappy, I was not irritated by all the Christmas music, to my surprise. People enjoying food and color and gifts and decorating was not painful to me.

And a little thought hovered near my head that said, there are still things to do for Rosalía. She is still in this world. Even though your actions are to comfort her on her way out, at least you still have actions to do. Soon there will be a time when I can't even go see her in the hospice.

But I'll think about that tomorrow.

Day 9
Wednesday, November 28

Today there was so much love swirling around Rosalía in great purple peace sign spirals.

Many found a moment of synchronicity. At one point, showing a friend a photo of Rosalía and her son in the play, *Ava*, the CD player began to play R. Carlos Nakai. I stopped moving and looked to my left. I didn't push play, I said to Marta. I didn't either, she said, but that's just what being with Rosalía is like.

It's Giving Tuesday and if you are still looking for a non-profit to make your wallet lighter, may I humbly recommend Scott's House hospice here in Santa Fe. They are compassionate giving personified.

In highly emotional situations, it is often the caring small things that people do on the side that bring a loving emotional response. I saw that happen several times with the good care all the staff and volunteers gave Rosalía today and all week. They all spoke to her kindly, looked her in the eye, were as gentle as they could be giving her a bath, and listened to friends and family with the patience of angels and bodhisattvas.

Family and friends continued to drop by, quietly telling her how much they love her, reading a story, getting a smile or an eyebrow raise, leaving her gifts of flowers, seeds, cards, photos.

One of the most profound gifts Rosalía received today was from herself. She had ordered a pair of boots before she got sick. Not any boots, mind you, but a pair of purple, faux-snakeskin, ankle-high, lace-up Doc Martens. They had just arrived in the mail and we put them on the altar. I see her kicking ass in the afterlife with those boots (in her beautiful way.)

Day 10
Wednesday November 29

Bardo for Dummies—that's what I read to Rosalía today.

That's not the real title of course; that's just what I've been calling it. A lot of people call it *The Tibetan Book of the Dead* and Robert Thurman has a very long, mellifluous and accurate translation of the title, but, it's really *Bardo for Dummies* as far as I'm concerned.

And that's not intended to be a derogatory title at all. It really is just a guide to help you remember what to do when you die. It's like a map, or a set of instructions on how to turn off the electricity before you change the light fixture. I think it's one of the most practical yet brilliant things I've read in my life.

At its core, there are five prayers which I nicknamed: the Guide, Helpers, Safety, Refuge, and The Betweens. And throughout, Thurman lets us know that this text—thoroughly researched by psychonauts during Tibet's centuries-long spiritual ascendance—is accessible to, and works well with, other spiritual traditions.

Rosalía's lifelong experience with past life regressions, (PLRs), as well as her own written experience sitting at the bedside of someone who was dying and reading the same text, encouraged me to look into it, and ask if she would like me to read it to her.

The morning was bright and beautiful, snow still crunching underfoot, the moon, bright every night no matter how small it's becoming. I sat with her this morning, it was just the two of us for a long time. I had printed out a copy of the Heart Sutra and left a plastic necklace of black skulls and bones from a recent Day of the Dead celebration snaking across it on her altar.

Someone was moving into the room next to her at the small hospice, so I closed the door to her room, which felt very odd. I hung a lavender beaded peace sign with bells on it on the door knob. I cleaned the altar, freshened the flowers. Then I moved some of the furniture so that I could sit both facing her and the beautiful view out the window to the west.

I leaned down close to her face and asked her again if she wanted me to read these prayers. She lifted up her eyebrows and left them there as she breathed deeply. This morning her breath was faster than it had been all week. I got the sense she was listening.

I began by facing each direction and thanking all the energy for being there for Rosalía and asking them to help me in reading for her.

The first prayer describes the Guide on this side and is a meditation on how the transition works.

Then there are four connected prayers: the invocation for beings, angels, buddhas and bodhisattvas to "come to this place" and help Rosalía begin to make the transition; the descriptions of the gods and consorts who will walk with her for protection; the recognition of beneficial lights and future parents; and a summary of all six between states.

If you've ever played Minecraft, think of the Nether. That's what the Bardo seems like to me reading this book. It's dark and fiery and full of potentially evil yet potentially beneficial entities, and you have to know which ones you can approach and which ones you should avoid. You can go to the Nether with others to protect you, but the rules of the rest of the world don't apply. Distance is very different in the Nether. There are also rare blocks and treasure that one can only find in the Nether.

Thurman includes in the translation exactly what you should be meditating on as you share these prayers next to a dying loved one. His descriptions are gorgeously colorful, which I thought Rosalía would especially enjoy. There is a diamond Buddha, and a ruby Buddha, and a rainbow Buddha, lights and marks and energies.

When I was done reading these prayers, I decided that was plenty for one day and maybe even for this lifetime. (Although *Bardo for Dummies* is a practice best done during life for the Tibetan people. In fact, it is recommended that you memorize these prayers so when death comes to you suddenly or slowly, you have them rehearsed.)

I stood up and closed the circle by thanking the four directions again.

Then we just sat there together, breathing for a while. I leaned close to her again and said that I hoped these prayers helped her. She didn't make any movement, but her face was more relaxed.

It wasn't long before her friend arrived. Marta carries a lot of joy for Rosalía. She greeted her and said it was lucky Rosalía was inside because it was as cold as a witch's tit outside. Rosalie raised her eyebrows and actually laughed. I mean, it was a very small laugh, but she smiled and she exhaled air.

I sat back on the chair and was astonished by a sudden thought. Transitioning from this life to the next, especially as an American, takes a lot of energy and a lot of focus. People shared jokes with her but I was giving her homework.

And I think Rosalía might just rather have fun.

Day 11
Thursday, November 30

Today the snow fell in Santa Fe like there was a sale on it. It snowed and snowed and snowed. I think I got eight inches. No one was getting up my hill today.

I missed going to the hospice to see Rosalía. I felt so far away from her today. I don't know what else I can do for her. Her friend Marta closed her chakras in a ceremony she had requested. I read her the prayers she could use as she walks through the next world.

Her loving friends and family have visited her and prayed for her, sent gifts and lit candles and shared stories. We heard from one of the caregivers today that she is alert and she is smiling a lot. She even sent herself the boots she needs for her new adventure. So, we are wondering, not without great compassion and love, Why is she still here? My guess is this: Rosalía is in her fourth act.

I love fourth acts. I love when a story is all finished and one more twist sends it spiraling like a roller coaster on an unexpected offshoot of track. I love it when my students find a fourth act in their work. I love it when my teachers have taught me you can go further, find a deeper place in the story.

Rosalía is not done with us. I don't think we should be done with her either. Yes, it will be so painful when she leaves. Grief will be our constant companion. We will regret things we should've said, wanted to say, maybe never should've said. We will miss her deeply. We will have all those emotions when she leaves.

But right now is a space in time like no other. A time when someone is still here. A moment when we can stop and ask ourselves, if I could talk to Rosalía one more time, what would she say? And you have that moment now.

One of my favorite Zen chants is the evening gatha:

Life and death are of supreme importance.
Time passes swiftly and opportunity is lost.
Awaken! Awake and take heed!
Do not squander your life.

Rosalía did not squander her life.

What is the one memory you have of a gift that Rosalía gave you? Ask her. Maybe she told you already this week.

For me, it was a past life regression she did for me that I have been remembering constantly. In it, I madly played a concert piano in a yellow satin dress (Chopin?) and the sound and feel of that experience has never left me, especially the keys touching the skin between my fingers and the vibration of the music up my arms. I'm not even sure I believe in past life regressions. And you know what she would say: That's OK.

To honor Rosalía, I decided as a bit of self-care that I would buy a bell that I could ring for zazen. Not a hand-bell because you can't control that, but a bowl from Nepal made of brass that you use a mallet to strike. Not so unlike piano keys. I used to have a bell that I got in Japan but I haven't seen it in years.

I walked into the Ark Bookstore yesterday to buy a bell. How is it possible that this bookstore that has been here in Santa Fe as long as I have, over 40 years, still smells exactly the same as when I first walked in? I remembered what Rosalía said to me when I first saw her in the hospital and bent down to hug her: You smell good, she said. You smell like you.

I rang bells and listened for the clearest tone that reverberated in the middle of my forehead. I gifted myself a golden bowl, a gold and white cushion, and a beautiful wooden mallet with suede on the end. And I will remember it was Rosalía who brought this bell to me.

Ringing a bell marks the beginning and end of a period of meditation but I have been using it for many reasons. I set the bell on my desk and rang it often just to clear the air. And clear my head. I rang it and spoke to Rosalía. I rang it to celebrate the snow. I rang it to practice ringing it.

I rang it for the pure joy of hearing it one more time.

Day 12
Friday December 1

I had this story written but was waiting to post it until about 10pm. I didn't get the chance.

I sat with Rosalía today in silence. Her breathing is fast but clear. She didn't wake when I entered her room.

The family has agreed for me to be called as soon as she passes, or if her passing looks imminent.

I'm waiting for a phone call. And I'm trying to think what this waiting is like. It is kind of like waiting for the birth of someone because you're on *their* timetable. It's also not unlike working on a film crew where you have to be ready to be up at all hours of the day and night, or at least be ready to move locations, print sides, or get a Diet Coke for the director's assistant.

What I'm doing to prepare:

Reading and listening to the audio version of *Bardo for Dummies.* That's the last time I'm gonna call it that because I am so enjoying the beautiful practicality of it. Robert Thurman calls his translation, *The Book of Natural Liberation.* And by the way, did you know Robert Thurman is Uma Thurman's father? If that isn't some kind of proof that we can choose our next lives, what is?

I have a backpack ready with my notebook journal; my very small book with the precepts written in it by me from my Jukai; a yellow, stained sutra card that I liberated from the San Francisco Zen temple circa 1980 and just found again yesterday; a small statue of Quan Yin for compassionate progress through the Bardo, wrapped in a scarf; a CD of the soundtrack to *City of Angels* (why?); and all my regular backpack stuff including a flashlight, toothbrush, lip gloss, a lighter, and a piece of caramel candy.

I have been wearing the same clothes for the last week, so I'm ready to go. This includes a purple sweater, a calf-length warm black skirt, black leggings, a purple amethyst necklace from Rosalía's, and a pair of silver heart earrings. When I'm home and working, I hang these clothes up but they're ready to go as soon as I go out the door. The black skirt is not something I wear often, but if I'm going to sit and meditate for a long period of time it is very flexible and very warm. The first day I chose it to wear to the hospice, I looked at it and said, Should I wear that Rosalía? And she said, Definitely.

I also have in the car a bag with my zafu—the black cushion I sit on for meditation—and my rakusu which in Zen terms is a baby robe. You wear it around your neck with a ring of bone. On the back is the stamp of my Zen lineage and teacher. I sewed pieces of cloth from my teacher and my family into the border. Did I sew a piece of cloth from Rosa? I hope so.

I have my phone charged at all times, and I have the phone numbers of people who will call me on override—in case I mute my phone and forget, their calls will still come through.

I make sure I eat at least one healthy meal a day and I'm drinking water. I limit my amount of alcohol because I might have to get in my car and drive at any minute. For self-care, I have a bag of chocolate pinwheel cookies.

I am continuing my other daily necessities with my work and my exercise as much as possible. I have very gracious clients and a boss who, luckily, gives me some flexibility.

The other thing I am doing in preparation is to be open. That's one of the last things Rosalía said to me. When she was still able to talk, her eyes opened wide to me after a moment of rest, and she said, I just died. I said you did? What was it like? And she said, Open. So open. And although I think of Rosalía as someone adept at traveling between past lives and current life, even in *Natural Liberation*, being there for someone when they pass to remind them how to choose to be free is something every single person can use, novice or adept.

I am open to the change in my life.
I am open to helping in whatever way I can.
I am open to the fact that I may not do things perfectly.
I am open to all the love that everyone is bringing.
I am open to feeling the grief of losing my friend.

But I might wait a little while to feel that last.

Day 12
Friday, December 1

Our dear Rosalía Triana flew away tonight on her way to her next adventure. I imagine her someday doing a past life regression—or whatever they will call it where she is now—and she'll remember us vividly as we will always remember her.

I've been thinking for several days that the last thing Rosalía taught me was how to be with someone as they were dying. As you know, she's a pretty great teacher; she makes you think like you're learning it on your own when really her wisdom was in letting you think that. She once taught me how to be a scripty in two hours at a coffee shop in Española and I went to work the next day for a feature film.

Therefore, please excuse my fumbling novice interpretation of Robert Thurman's incredible translation of *The Book of Natural Liberation*, aka, *The Tibetan Book of the Dead*, aka *Bardo for Dummies*. As a disclaimer, please know that if you've just heard about Rosalía's passing, this writing might seem irreverent to you, but no disrespect. And per Rosalía, no apologies.

I had visited Rosalía in the afternoon, and was not surprised when I got the call at 7:30 pm from the hospice number. I had made plans with the family to be there after she passed. I had just put a fresh coat of nail polish on my right hand. Girl, I joked, your timing needs work.

The caregiver on duty let me know that Rosalía had just then passed; I was the first person she was calling. I wrote the date and time in purple ink on a Post-it note: Nov 1, 7:30 pm, but realized it was December. I let them know I would be there as soon as possible.

My first thoughts were, *Good girl! You did it. You are now free from suffering. I'm so proud of you!* I planned to leave grieving for tomorrow.

My mind then turned anxious. As described in *Natural Liberation*, there is a small window of time after the person dies when their soul is still within or near their subtle energetic body, and given the right instruction, they can sidestep the horrors of the Bardo or "between." I wasn't sure if I would get there in time so I began talking to Rosalía while I quickly put a topcoat on my nails, otherwise I'd be dragging nail polish all over my clothes.

In a mild panic, I forgot everything I'd read in the last week, and called out: *Go toward the light, Rosalía!* as if I were Phoebe in *Friends*. I corrected myself and said, *Go toward the bright light, the clear, bright light! That's you. You made that light and you need to recognize that it is you.*

I fed my cat, turned off the space heater, jumped in the car and warmed it up. I backed out of my snowy driveway and my wheels spun. I backed out a second time and made it up the hill without an issue.

I continued talking to Rosalía. I said, *Listen. You need to know that you have died. You have left your body. It may seem cold, you may be confused, but just remember your own spiritual path that you just left. Think about the Virgin of Guadalupe, she's there to guide you. I have to drive now, but I will be there very soon.*

As I drove down the shiny icy streets, I aimed a thought at her and said in a regular voice, This is ridiculous, right? I heard her answer, Well…? as if she were shrugging her shoulders. What the fuck? Let's do it anyway!

When I got to her room, I nodded at who I presumed to be the on-call nurse, dropped my heavy backpack on a chair and walked up to Rosalía's bed. She looked the same as when I'd left her that afternoon. But of course she wasn't moving. There was no breath.

I bent down and said in a strong voice:

Dear Rosalía, you Beautiful Girl! It's Melissa. I love you! You have just died and this might be confusing to you, but you're very safe—you have people to help you where you are and I'll help you, too. We'll say some prayers together. Don't be afraid.

I watched her chest and thought I saw her heart beating. I looked around behind me at the nurse and the caregiver who was standing in the doorway and I asked, She is dead, right?

They confirmed she was.

I stood up then and said hello to the nurse, took off my

coat and gloves. We exchanged names. She said they
would wait to call the transport until I was done and to
take my time. Then they left me alone.

I realized at this time that, according to *Natural Liberation*,
her soul might not be near her body, but could be anywhere in the room. I looked around Everything seemed
the same as the afternoon, except that there was no motor-
ized sound of her oxygen tank. The day before, still able to
communicate, she had refused oxygen.

I leaned down and looked at Rosalía's face carefully. She
was peaceful, but her light was not there anymore. I put
my hand on her forehead; it was still warm.

I opened a sacred circle by inviting each of the directions
in. I faced the window a little light-headed and said, Is this
north? No, said the north, that's west. I turned and faced
north.

I said my first invitation to the north to be there with me
and Rosalía but no words came out; they were caught
in my throat. I gestured to the north to come in and got
control of my emotion and was able to speak the words. I
turned in each direction and invited them as well.

Then I sat down on the tall chair facing both Rosalía and
the window and began reading out loud the prayers from
The Book of Natural Liberation for one who has just died.
Parts of those prayers are so amazingly direct:

Hey, noble one! Now you have arrived at what is called "death." You are going from this world to the beyond. You are not alone; it happens to everyone.

Hey, noble one! At this time when your mind and body are parting ways, pure reality manifests in subtle, dazzling visions, vividly experienced, naturally frightening and worrisome, shimmering like a mirage on the plains in autumn. Do not fear them. Do not be terrified! Do not panic! …they cannot hurt you. You cannot die.

When I finished reading each prayer three times, I also chanted the Heart Sutra, which is the essence of wisdom and healing—one I've been chanting since I was in my 20s. This chant brought me great emotion. Part of it is translated:

Gone, gone, gone beyond, gone beyond beyond.

I looked at my watch. It had been exactly an hour since she passed. I sincerely hoped being there with her helped her in some way. She might still be wandering in the between, but in my heart, I felt like she was already liberated. Still, I will speak the prayers for each day as instructed. Because this is as much practice and healing for me as it is beneficial to her.

I told her, *I'm going to say goodbye to your body now, Rosalía. Thank you for being in this life with me.* I moved close to her and bent down again, putting a kiss on my fingers and putting my fingers on her forehead.

This time her skin was cool.

I closed the circle starting with the west, and moving backwards, sending thanks and prayers, shedding tears.

The on-call nurse came to the door and I let her know we had had our time together. She said she would call the transport to take Rosalía back to Española. She left and I stood facing the window, reciting the names of her brothers and sisters, her good friends in Española, our friends in writing class and film school, all I could remember.

As I turned to leave the room, I felt a presence behind me, but it was sweet. I felt a ribbon in my hand, the kind they tie to a helium balloon, red with tiny folds in it. In my mind's eye, I saw a purple balloon following me as I held the string that was tied to it.

Rosalía, I said, *you can follow me around the hospice, but once they take your body to Española, I'm going to let you go. You need to find your way on your own. I'll say prayers for you every day. You cannot linger here.*

When the transport came, they covered her in a beautiful warm Native blanket. As they passed through the hallway, the caregiver rang the gong on the altar three times. I bowed and followed the stretcher out into the cold, bright, moonlit night.

As I write this in the wee hours of the morning, I remember the moon rising, the bottom half a beautiful circle towards the Earth, the top, a hazy smudge of sky and stars. I feel she is out there, riding high among the planets, having her last gorgeous laugh with us.

For me, she was just a star in disguise.

Rosalía Triana - A Life Story

by Robert Tomlinson

Rosalía Triana was born on Friday the 13th, in December, 1946, in Parma, Ohio. She left the Midwest in the '70s heading anywhere else with her friend, Julia, in a VW bus named Shirley.

She eventually landed in Cerrillos, New Mexico. It was here, with a like-minded group of people where she built a pit house. She treasured this time on what is known as, "The Land." During these days, she taught theater at Santa Fe Alternative School, where she met her son, Martin.

The early '80s called her to New York City. It was the height of the punk rock/new wave/experimental theater movement. She was involved with the radical theater group, "La Mama." It was also in New York that she honed her skill as a master tarot reader and past life regressionist. She appeared in several notable films such as *Cotton Club*, *Moonstruck*, and the cult classic, *Convoy*. She grew tired of the pace, coldness and claustrophobia of the city and returned to her beloved Northern New Mexico in the early '90s.

Upon her return, she decided to pursue her master's degree in Chicano/Chicana theater. At the time she was living in El Valle, near Peñasco, and she commuted to UNM in Albuquerque three times a week.

She succeeded; she was like that.

Shortly after, she became Theater Director at Northern New Mexico Community College between 2001 and 2013. It was here that she realized she was finally "home." Rosalía brought the theater up to modern standards and helped to create a community of incomparable artists: musicians, theater people, painters, photographers, sculptors—offering a safe place for people to express themselves to the fullest.

Rosalía had a long history of creating and supporting performing arts in New Mexico. If you were involved in any of these organizations, you know the dedication she had:

Moving Arts Española, LiveArts Santa Fe (board member), Mel Patch Artspace, TAC Club, Teatro Paraguas, SAG, Española Main Street Theater (co-founder), Northern New Mexico Community College, and New Mexico Filmmakers Intensive where her screenplay, "Epi's Dilemma," was one of the few chosen to be produced. You can watch it on YouTube.

Rosalía recognized the transitional power of her craft and found the celebration of community, transformation and healing in every project. She encouraged people to take the first step in understanding their story. If you knew her, you have a Rosalía story of your own.

Rosalía is survived by her son, Martin Barela (Bernice), and grandson, Travis Barela; siblings Mary Traina,

Elizabeth Leary, Terry Safranek (Kenneth), Patty Traina, Michael Traina (Deborah), and Steve Traina; and longtime co-conspirator, Robert Tomlinson, as well as several nieces, nephews, and five million members of her extended family she created wherever she went.

The family would like to extend thanks to Marta Uribe, Carolina Jaramillo-Salazar at Scott's House, and a special thanks to Melissa J White.

A Celebration of Life Event will be held Saturday, January 13, 2024, from 4 to 6 pm at Moving Arts Española. The public is invited. Please RSVP to info@movingartsespano-la.org.

A party in Rosalía's honor will happen in the spring.

The family requested that in lieu of flowers, you may make a donation in Rosalía's name to Scott's House Community Hospice and Respite, or Moving Arts Española, or any other organization that you think is doing work to better the human condition.

Dime con quién andas, y te diré quién eres.
"Tell me who you walk with and I will tell you who you are."

– Spanish proverb

Thank you

To all of Rosalía's family: Steve, Terry, Patty Jean, Michael, Elizabeth, Martin, and Robert, Erika, and Marta: thank you for your encouragement, support, and the wonderful way we are keeping Rosalía's memory alive in love and laughter. To Sunday Writers Margaret and Áine: thank you for the days of the four of us writing together; I will treasure them. Thank you, Robert Thurman, for the vibrant translation of *The Tibetan Book of the Dead*. A heartfelt thank you to Rosalía's caregivers at Scott's House and at Presbyterian Española Hospital for your compassionate care. To all of Rosalía's friends and her one-time magical acquaintances I had not met before these two weeks: it was a joy to meet you and a revelation to see how special she made us all feel.

Also by Melissa J White:

Angel Someone (Amazon, 2010)
Dizzy Sushi (Tres Chicas Books, 2013)

More at Facing-Pages.com